KIM YORK

SUCCESSFUL COACHING

The Ultimate Guide on How to Start a Coaching Business, Learn Powerful Tips on How to Build Your Coaching Skills and Start Your Own Coaching Business

Descrierea CIP a Bibliotecii Naționale a României
KIM YORK
  SUCCESSFUL COACHING. The Ultimate Guide on How
to Start a Coaching Business, Learn Powerful Tips on How to
Build Your Coaching Skills and Start Your Own Coaching
Business / Kim York – Bucharest: Editura My Ebook, 2021
  ISBN

KIM YORK

SUCCESSFUL COACHING

The Ultimate Guide on How to Start a Coaching Business, Learn Powerful Tips on How to Build Your Coaching Skills and Start Your Own Coaching Business

My Ebook Publishing House
Bucharest, 2021

KIM YORK

SUCCESSFUL COACHING

TABLE OF CONTENTS

INTRODUCTION

When it comes to providing effective solutions for the client, the coaching techniques are a little unique and very much focused on getting the client to where he or she wants to be within a stipulated period of time. Get all the info you need here.

CHAPTER 1

PROVIDE EFFECTIVE SOLUTIONS
TO YOUR CLIENTS

Synopsis

The idea behind the exercise would be to challenge the client to reach heights never before thought of possible with the help and guidance of the coaching exercise.

The Basics

The coach would ideally want to understand the vision that the client has and then create and outline of steps that the client will be able to follow to effectively get the vision from that stage to reality. In some cases, the inclusion of inspiring tips may be needed to get the client excited about reaching the end goal faster.

This exercise would also require the coaching session to include helping the client to discover the life currently lead in more depth and explore changes so that personal development and accomplishments both professionally and personally can be made. Making the client accountable and helping the client reach his or her true potential is the key to developing the growth factor.

There is also the active participation of the coach in helping the client to increase the creativity, productive and effectiveness levels in tackling tasks set in the quest to reach the end goal, as projected. Teaching the client skills that will help in reaching the goal with a bigger difference and to accelerate the choices made in terms of career choices and personal choices is also something the coach would have to try and incorporate into the training sessions. Helping the client shed any fears and hesitations that are causing the current slump should also be part to the coaching exercise, as this too will help the client be a more overall effective person.

CHAPTER 2

ASKING THE RIGHT QUESTION
TO YOUR AUDIENCE

Synopsis

One of the more effective ways of getting the audience to participate and interact within the coaching session would be to incorporate the questions and answers session within the framework of the session.

What To Ask

However if this is not done with careful thought and planning, the questions chosen could end up causing problems, when there is little or no response from the audience.

Questions are a great way to gauge the attention span of the listening audience. This will give the coach a clear indication on whether the session is benefiting the audience and how much the audience has been able to grasp so far. With the incorporation of questions into the presentation, the coach will also be able to get the audience out of the listening only mode and into the active participation mode. This is important as it will also help the audience to put into practice the issues being presented.

Ideally, the questions sessions should be designed around a few important ideas, some of which would have to include the exercise of bringing out the potential of an individual or a member of the team within the audience, creating more meaningful interactions with the audience and the exercise of building a strong and good rapport with the listening audience. All these are meant to ensure the coaching session is beneficial to the audience in creating the awareness required to get the audience to the next level in their respective lives and careers.

Correctly designed questions, will also get the audience seriously contemplating and thinking about the presentation made within the frame of the coaching session, thus helping them to mull over the information and share any doubts or queries they made have immediately. The questions should ideally be designed, to help tap into the audience perspective on the topic presented and the relevancy it is expected to play in their lives.

CHAPTER 3

GETTING COMMITMENT
BY ASSIGNING TASK/HOMEWORK

Synopsis

Making a presentation is often a comparatively easy part of coaching and most coaches find this relatively simple when compared to the other connecting follow up exercises incorporated into the overall exercise of ensuring the message is delivered, understood and practiced by the audience.

Why Homework?

The assigning of tasks and homework is meant to help both parties ensure the best of the session has been absorbed and understood. This format will allow the coach to have a better idea of exactly how well the coaching session has been able to impact the minds of the listening audience. It will also give the coach some perspective on the ways the information delivered will be used in the individual lives of the participating audience. Ensuring the information presented at the coaching session is well received and used in the desired way is also another reason for the tasks or homework necessity. At this point the coach will be able to view the effectiveness of the coaching sessions and make improvements or adjustments should there be a need for it.

It will also provide a good platform for the audience to put into practical use the information gained at the session in a more committed form. Helping to develop a more independent use of the information learnt is also something that can be displayed through the work produced based on the tasks and assignments given. It will also allow the audience to display some level of independence in how the information is to be incorporated into their lives based on their own perspective and understanding.

Should the use of the information learnt be displayed in a manner that is contrary to its original presentation, the coach will be able to address this as it would show up in the task or homework done.

CHAPTER 4

MAKING YOUR COACHING
SESSION ENTERTAINING

Synopsis

Often attending coaching sessions can be quite a challenge, especially if the subject matter is rather boring and takes a lot of mental and physical effort on the part of the participating parties. However, there are ways a coach can use to ensure the participants are having an enjoyable time at the sessions.

Don't Be A Bore

The following are some of the ways to make a coaching session entertaining and interesting:

• A coach who wants to ensure the sessions are effective and entertaining in some respect would have to work by certain attitudes. There should be a sense of determination, and the ability to "feel" the needs of the audience, especially if there is a difficult presentation to be understood. Going about this in a creative and intelligent way would help to keep all parties working well and smoothly. Therefore being constantly mindful of the "atmosphere" would help.

• Relevancy is also another aspect that the coach would have to look into. Being able to ensure the material is designed to suit the audience and done so in a fashion that would come across as interesting and full of injections of movements and suitable body language antics should be considered.

• Good coaches usually know how and when to inject a good story telling session into the coaching exercise. Most people love to listen to stories and it is even better if the story chosen is relative to an event that has actually taken place. The more real the story content, the better the audience is able to connect to the story telling session.

- The ability to laugh and not take things too seriously is also another important characteristic to have in order to be an effective coach. Injecting humor into the presentation material and then expressing it well will keep the audience excited and interested in the presentation

CHAPTER 5

CREATE A POWERFUL PRESENTATION SLIDES

Synopsis

Part of a good coaching presentation exercise has to include some slide presentation sections. However these sessions should be well designed and planned to ensure they are of the best quality and style as the audience attention span is the important factor to be able to attract and hold.

Catch Their Eye

The following are some tips on elements to consider when creating a powerful presentation of slides for the coaching session:

• Keeping it simple is perhaps the most important factor to consider. Coaching session are already comprised of a lot of material to absorb, therefore designing the slides to portray a very simple message with each slide is important. This will help the audience not to feel overwhelmed. Also, avoid too much color and distorted images, as this may cause confusion to the audience.

• Limiting the bullet points and text is also another important element to consider. Too much written matter being shown on the slide would only render the content boring and another ineffective style used to exhaust the brain and concentration levels of the audience even more. Shorter and simpler presentations would be better welcomed.

• Limit the transitions and builds that use the animation platform. This should be judiciously used, as ideally, it is not necessary to include these animations in every single slide. Boredom quickly sets in, if there are too many slides in succession using the same style to present the material. Using no more than two or three types of transition effects without the same effects between all the slides would be a better style to go with.

• The quality of graphics chosen should also be higher. This will reflect well on the coach and the material used. The choice of graphics is important in maintaining certain quality level for the overall presentation.

CHAPTER 6

PROVIDE STEP BY STEP GUIDE

Synopsis

Coaching effectively is not something that can be done without the relevant effort put into designing the material and the presentation style. There are also other aspects that should be taken into consideration, if the coaching session is to be an overall success.

Make A Plan

The following are some areas to consider in providing a step by step guild to how to get things done effectively so that the best coaching sessions are featured:

Being able to coach confidently should be the priority of any step by step guide. Confidence is a prerequisite of effective coaching. If the presenter is confident in to the material and the style to be used, the audience will be able to better accept the content being presented mainly based on the confidence in which it is being presented.

Building a niche would also be another area to consider for the success of being able to stay relevant in this competitive field. Taking the time and effort to create this niche will effectively get the coach noticed and thus perhaps create the platform for this created interest to contribute further to the popularity of the coach and the coaching sessions and material.

In this very competitive arena, it may sometimes be prudent to make a presentation to the potential client with a fairly detailed outline within a trial session arranged for viewing. Using this opportunity to push the coaching session as effective and something worth exploring should be part of the presentation made at the trial session.

Designing the coaching session to include some active participation from the audience will also help to break the monotony of the sessions. Incorporating this interactive module will also help the coach to gauge the understanding capacity of the audience and just how much they have been able to gain from the sessions.

CHAPTER 7

TRACK YOUR CLIENT'S PROGRESS

Synopsis

Part of being a good and effective coach, is to be able to gauge the progress of the client periodically to ensure everyone and everything is on the right track. This will help the coach make the necessary adjustments if there is a need to change or improve on the current program being used.

Keep Track

The following are some tips on the areas that should be considered if the coach in concerned about the client's progress.

• Setting goals that are customized would be a good place to start. Questionnaires should be designed to ask the same questions in varying intervals as the answers given, will reflect the progress made with each consequent module presented.

• Tracking the responses of each client individually using the answers provided by the client in the questionnaires will also show the different facets of the clients understanding of the material and may even present some surprising information that could be used to explore other elements within coaching sessions. This kind of assessments done periodically will also help the coach to decide on consequent material being used and it relevancy and beneficial values the material brings to the client.

• The tracking system will also allow the coach to review the effectiveness of the sessions already attended by the client and decide if the current program chosen, is contributing positively to the end goal first decided at the onset of the coaching session. The will also allow the coach to review the clients responses easily and as often as needed, because the information provided at the assessment, will usually be stored for further scrutiny.

• These tracking sessions also allows both parties to review the progress being made and to use this as a motivational tool to further encourage the client to reach for bigger and better goals.

CHAPTER 8

MOTIVATE YOUR CLIENT TO GREATER BREAKTHROUGH

Synopsis

Motivation is the key to getting things done, and with the right motivational tactics, it is possible to get anything done with the right amount of enthusiasm and urgency.

Help Them Along

The following are some tips on how to get the client to be motivated enough to strive for greater breakthroughs:

- Once the client has been able to achieve the original goal, it easier to encourage the client to try for something a little more challenging. When the client is willing, then the coach would have to design new formats that should include some motivational exercises, to get the client in the right frame of mind, so that the focus can now be on achieving greater breakthroughs.

- There should also be some level of care when it comes to motivating the client to achieve further breakthroughs. This is to ensure and protect the client form possible burnout. Therefore coaching the client to focus on one goal at a time should be part of the encouraging technique used. Making sure that the client really committed and the reasons for the commitment are legitimate would help the coach design the appropriate motivational exercise to encourage the greater breakthrough.

- "Selling" the concept to the client, is another way to get the client interested and motivated enough to push boundaries and strive for more and higher achievements. There is always the excitement that is usually felt at the onset of the endeavor, but the motivation used should be able to keep the excitement to carry right through until the goal is achieved. The level of excitement the coach is able to display will eventually have some effect on the client, thus garnering the heightened interest levels which can then be used to focus on making further breakthroughs.

CHAPTER 9

APPLY PERSUASIVE SPEAKING TECHNIQUES

Synopsis

Being able to make a good presentation will garner the appropriate level of interest in the subject matter, however doing the same thing in a persuasive manner will not only garner the attention of the audience but till also get the audience to commit to the endeavor completely.

Hold Their Attention

The following are some ways to get the audience to be adequately committed through persuasive speaking techniques:

- Body language is a great way to connect with the audience. When the appropriate body language is used, the connection with the audience can be heightened and thus create the perfect platform for the coaching session to be more productive and successful. People generally respond to certain positive body language skills, and it would be good for the individual to master these techniques and incorporate them into the coaching sessions. Hand gestures, eye contact, and other expressive movements will all add to the overall impact to the speaking exercise to add to the persuasiveness of the exercise.

- Being well versed on the subject to be presented at the coaching session, will also contribute to the client being impressed enough to be persuaded to commit. The influence the coach will be able to have over the audience will be based on the perception the audience has on the quality of the material and also on the persuasive tone and presentation style used.

Credibility of the information and the logic in which it is presented will all point to the persuasive element the coach incorporates into the session.

- When designing the material for the presentation, the coach should include strong opening and closing points to persuade the audience to commit to the endeavor totally. These two parts of the entire presentation are very important and good opportunities to be persuasive.

CHAPTER 10

OVER DELIVER YOUR PROGRAMS
WITH ADDED VALUE CONTENT/PRODUCTS

Synopsis

In the quest to outdo the competition, most people look for ways that they can impress the client without actually having to commit to anything other than what has already been promised. This of course is not a very effective way of going about making the client happy and standing out in the service provided.

Do It Right

Although the general idea for most businesses is to be able to cut cost as much as possible, this should not be done at the expense of the value being given to the client. Although shallow value delivery has become the norm for most people, this would give the individual the opportunity to stand out with added value content and product which would certainly be a pleasant surprise for the client.

If the individual is able to see the potential in providing programs with added value content, then the quest to do so will be much easier and definitely motivation enough to look into this angle. This will eventually be seen in the quality of the programs presented and it will be impressive enough for the client to not only firmly commit, but to also continue to be an important client for the individual. Therefore, the habit of over delivering on anything should be incorporated into any design created, as this will always have the added benefit of impressing the client. Clients will be impressed at the effort and commitment of the individual toward giving his or her best to the entire exercise, thus making it easier for the individual to get repeat business and recommendations.

Over delivering on anything need not necessarily be about providing a costly added benefit without charge or providing a lot of freebies. This idea of over delivering can come in simple forms such as follow up services that are equally impressive, added attention lavished on the client and being totally committed to addressing all the clients' queries and simply providing the support that may not seem necessary but would speak volumes to the client.

CHAPTER 11

TRANSITION FROM A COACH
TO AN ENTREPRENEUR

Synopsis

The following are some guidelines to follow if the individual is interested in making the transition from coach to entrepreneur and effective and monetarily beneficial endeavor.

The Basics

Being sufficiently excited and enthusiastic about the idea, would help in getting the individual to consider the transition in a positive light. Once this becomes an interesting and enticing option to consider, the coach can then be made to explore the various ways this can be made into a reality.

The very important ingredient of optimism is a very important element to have as this will help to fuel the excitement and energy required to stick to creating the circumstances whereby the coach will eventually become a successful entrepreneur. However, some caution should be exercise here, so that the enthusiasm and excitement does not cause the coach to have unreasonable and unrealistic expectations.

This is rather unrealistic view, could eventually lead to the probable deflation in the excitement and energy that was initially very much the focal point of the entire idea behind the expansion exercise.

With the excited mindset, the coach can then set about embarking on the various exercises such as being a part of as many networking opportunities as possible to promote the business angle of the coaching expertise, getting other like minded individual's to form a joint venture program, make presentations when ever invited to do so, or actually initialing the invitation to make a presentation, getting interested parties to put the word out about the services currently enjoyed thus effectively becoming a good advertising tool for the coach, and many other activities that would help to expand the actual coaching sessions in to a successful business opportunity.

CHAPTER 12

WAYS TO RAISE CAPITAL FOR YOUR BUSINESS

Synopsis

There are a lot of ways to explore for the exercise of raising adequate amounts of money for business capital purposes. However with the wide array of possibilities available, comes the confusion in knowing which style would be considered suitable and thus should be adopted by the individual.

Your Options

Launching a new business, expanding an existing business or simply getting the current business running smoothly, all require the assistance of adequate capital, and this is often a point of contention and difficulty for those who lack finances. The following are some ideas on how to raise capital for the business:

• The most popular source to look towards would be that of family and friends. Creating an impacting presentation and then presenting it with confidence and energetic enthusiasm will help to entice and attract the attention and interest of the listening audience, thus hopefully be enough to get them to invest enthusiastically.

• If the individual wants to take a more professional approach to garnering some capital, more formal sources can be sought, such as lending houses which would include banks, capital investors, finance houses and other legitimate sources. However, getting financial help from such sources would require the individual to present a very official and feasible working paper on the business venture intended. This is to ensure the financial assistance will be considered in a positive light. The working paper should be done in a very professional manner, befitting to the platform it is to be presented at.

- Other ways of raising capital for the business may include taking on partners. With the formation of the partnership, there would be an added source of financing possibilities and also the additional expertise to form a stronger product package to be presented to the eventual client. The addition of the other party into the partnership will ideally come with enough capital investment, to ensure the expansion of the business would be made possible.

CHAPTER 13

BUILD A REMARKABLE BRAND

Synopsis

Branding building is very important as it is supposed to be the clear representation of the company or the business endeavor being promoted. Effective brand building will help to bring the items being promoted to the forefront of the clients' attention, thus creating the opportunity for both the merchant and the client to come to a mutual and beneficial partnership.

Make Something Great

The following are some points on how to build a remarkable brand:

- Image is very important to the brand building concept. The right image used will ensure the desired attraction and interest to the material being promoted. This is important, as the target audience is usually overwhelmed with choices, that it would be hard to choose the individual's brand, if it is not marketed in a style that is able to capture the attention of the client immediately.

- Accessibility is also another important point to consider when addressing the brand building exercise. Often the promotions for the brand building exercise, takes up the entire focus of all involved, that the easy accessibility to the material or product being promoted is over looked. This is very frustrating for the client, who would like to commit to the brand, but has no recourse to do so, thus forcing the client to look elsewhere.

- In the actual designing phase of the brand building, it would be wise to explore all the various tools available in the market place today to ensure the best are used to create an attention grabbing campaign. This would include identifying the best colors, designs, captions, characters and anything else that should ideally be included in the end promotional campaign. Consistency in making the promotional campaign a memorable one is important as this will work as the ideal pulling factor to ensure the overall success of the end results.

CHAPTER 14

DEVELOP EFFECTIVE MARKETING STRATEGIES

Synopsis

Every business endeavor requires a certain amount of market planning, and each step requires the undivided attention of the individual in order to ensure all the correct decisions are made to strategically position the business for success.

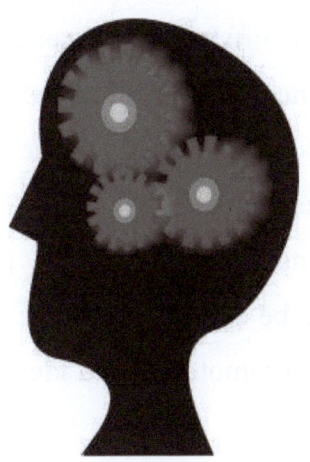

Create Strategies

The following are some tips on how to develop effective marketing strategies to ensure the success of the business endeavor:

Taking the time to identify and suitable describe the company's unique selling point will help when it comes to promoting the company's services to the potential client.

The promotional material used can focus heavily on this selling point to ensure the client is sufficiently impressed and thus be more inclined to make a commitment. Being able to create the adequate amount of awareness will be a helpful marketing strategy.

Defining and identifying the target audience, should also another marketing strategy that could be explored. This will help to design the other connective parts of the presentation material to entice and gain the client's attention.

If the marketing strategy is well planned around this information, it would be easy to encourage the client to commit, as the material being promoted would ideally be what the client needs or wants.

This will ultimately be the defining factor of exactly how good the strategy being used, will eventually ensure the supporting information is designed to create the ideal package for the client.

Defining the marketing tools to be used is also another way of creating suitable marketing strategies for the business. With the relevant amount of research done, the individual should be able to identify the suitable tools for the advertising platform that will eventually be use to launch the business entity and reach the prospective clients effectively.

These strategies could include the use of the internet, advertising campaigns, direct marketing, public relations and any other ways that would create awareness for the business.

CHAPTER 15

ADVERTISING IS IMPORTANT TO GET NOTICED

Synopsis

Creating awareness is one of the most effective ways of getting the client's attention and consequential commitment towards any endeavor. Therefore, in the quest to create this very important awareness aspect, the individual would explore the opportunities provided for, by the advertising angles available.

Put Your Name Out

Advertising is a great tool to use when there is a need to connect the prospective client to the source producing the product, service or materials needed. Being the ideal platform for informing the client of the various positive points that can be enjoyed with the use of the said product, service or material, the

53

individual would effectively be able to make a success of the business endeavor, without actually having to physically sell to the client. Advertising creates the ideal opportunity for the company to reach a larger target audience with relative ease.

Advertising is also beneficial in keeping the current customers and clients still interested in the product, service or material being advertised.

A lot of businesses, seem to forget to tap into the already existing market as they wrongly assume, that once the customer signs on to the commitment, there is no further need to promote the qualities of the business any longer, wrongly thinking the customer is already well informed and impressed with the results the business entity offers.

However changing this mindset is important, to the survival of the business, as advertising can also be used to refocus the possible waning attention and interest of the client back to its original enthusiasm. At some point loyal customers would also like to be wooed and considered special enough to be privy to the advertising campaign being promoted.

There is a lot of competition in the market place, to garner the attention of clients; therefore, equal focus would be given to the advertising part of the business to encourage the awareness factor, so that the eventual positive results can be garnered for the furtherance of the business entity.

CHAPTER 16

EXPAND YOUR BUSINESS TO CYBERSPACE

Synopsis

A lot of business entities today are exploring the possibility of expanding their business and getting the attention needed for this through the cyberspace platform. There is a lot of interest in this particular way of getting the business entity recognized, as it is done on a much larger scale than any other more conventional method.

Use The Web

The following are some of the contributing factors that are currently encouraging businesses to seek the cyberspace exposure, as a suitable platform for creating effective awareness:

• Perhaps the most obvious reason for this option being explored is the main advantage of being able to reach a wider target audience. With the use of the cyberspace platform, the infinite possibilities of being able to reach anyone with an internet connection is rivaled by no other advertising tool. Such advertising possibilities are hard to be able to guarantee but with the cyberspace tool, this is no longer an issue.

• There is also the cost factor when it comes to advertising, which is almost always expensive. With the use of the cyberspace tool, this cost factor will no longer be a negative element that curbs the ability of the business to reach the target audience. Comparatively, using the cyberspace platform as the ideal advertising tool, is definitely a lot cheaper and easier to explore and implement.

• Another attractive reason to use the cyberspace as a business expansion tool would be manpower or lack of it. In considering any business expansion, the individual would have to factor in the need to have all the supporting equipment and the work force in place, to handle all the additional work. With the cyberspace tool, this is not only not necessary but it may also allow the individual to give up the current workforce already in service, as the cyberspace tools will be able to adequately create and handle any incoming business for the individual.

Wrapping Up

Coaching effectively and setting up an effective coaching system can be a tricky task. With the use of some of these simple tips though coaching someone effectively can be made easy. Take this information in and begin being a good coach to your clients today.

Printed by Libri Plureos GmbH in Hamburg, Germany